✦ TITLE PAGE ◀

Pursuing Wisdom and Godliness

A 30-Day Challenge for Men Who Refuse to Drift

By Marty Bergey

✦ DEDICATION ✦

This book is dedicated to the men who choose conviction over comfort, truth over trend, and faith over fear.

To the warriors who stand firm when the world wavers, who lead their homes, guard their hearts, and refuse to compromise when it counts.

To the fathers raising children to know the voice of God, and to the brothers who walk beside each other through both victories and valleys.

And most of all, to the men who are still in the fight, the ones who stumble, rise, and keep pursuing wisdom and godliness with all their hearts.

May this book remind you that your strength isn't found in perfection but in persistence, and that God is never done shaping the man who refuses to quit.

✦ BEFORE YOU BEGIN ✦

This book is not a book to rush through. It is a conversation with God that unfolds over time.

Before reading each day, pause. Take a breath. Ask the Holy Spirit to open your heart and speak through what you read.

These devotions are not instructions to follow but invitations to listen — to let wisdom form inside you through reflection and obedience.

Stroll. God meets those who move with purpose, not haste.

✦ INTRODUCTION ✦

Every generation faces a decision: to drift with culture or to anchor in truth.

Drifting feels easy — it demands nothing and promises everything. But anchors are forged in struggle, and that is where godliness grows.

This book was written for men who want more than good intentions. It is for those who want to live with conviction, lead with integrity, and stand tall in a world that bends easily.

Each day is intentional but straightforward — a Scripture, a short parable, and a challenge to live out what you believe. You will not find perfection here, only direction.

The goal is not to finish quickly but to finish faithfully.

Take these 30 days and the seven bonus days that follow to slow down, dig deep. Be still, God will shape the man He designed you to be.

✦ TABLE OF CONTENTS ✦

Front Matter

1. Title Page
2. Copyright Page
3. Dedication
4. Before You Begin
5. Introduction
6. Table of Contents

Main Devotionals

Day 1 – Jesus Defeated Death So You Can Live

Day 2 – Truth Is Not Relative

Day 3 – Guard Your Heart

Day 4 – Strength in Humility

Day 5 – Discipline Over Desire

Day 6 – The Company You Keep

Day 7 – Faith Under Fire

Day 8 – Purpose in the Pain

Day 9 – Freedom Requires Faith

Day 10 – Words Build Worlds

Day 11 – When God Says Wait

Day 12 – The Weight of Integrity

Day 13 – Wisdom in the Wilderness

Day 14 – Anchored in Truth

Day 15 – We Are Pilgrims, Not Residents

Day 16 – Stay on the Narrow Way

Day 17 – Scripture Ahead of Its Time

Day 18 – We All Fall Short

Day 19 – Conviction Is Contagious

Day 20 – Defiant Hope

Day 21 – Lessons in Every Season

Day 22 – The Power of Quiet Strength

Day 23 – Forgiven to Forgive

Day 24 – The Strength of Servanthood

Day 25 – Guard Your Mind

Day 26 – Faith That Moves Mountains

Day 27 – Courage in the Fire

Day 28 – The Power of God's Word

Day 29 – Faith Over Fear

Day 30 – Finish the Race

✨ The Pursuit Continues — 7 Bonus Devotionals

Day 31 – *The Pursuit Continues*

Press on in faith — the journey does not end when the book does.

Day 32 – *A Man of Integrity*

Stand firm when no one is watching; your character is your legacy.

Day 33 – *The Battle Within*

Every man fights between flesh and spirit — choose who wins daily.

Day 34 – *Purpose Over Pleasure*

Find fulfillment not in feeling good but in living for what's eternal.

Day 35 – *Faith That Endures*

Endurance is not about perfection — it is about finishing strong.

Day 36 – *God's Timing Is Perfect*

Wait well; what God delays, He develops.

Day 37 – *A Life Worth Remembering*

Live for the Master's "Well done," not the world's applause.

Letters to My Brothers

(A Word from My Heart to Yours)

Letter 1 – To the Man Who's Just Beginning

For the brother standing at the starting line of faith and purpose.

Letter 2 – To the Husband Who Feels Tired

For the man carrying the weight of love, work, and quiet burdens.

Letter 3 – To the Father Raising Warriors

For dads, building courage and faith in their sons.

Letter 4 – To the Father Raising Daughters

For men learning to lead with gentleness and strength.

Letter 5 – To the Man Fighting Quiet Battles

For those who struggle in silence but refuse to give up.

Letter 6 – To the Young Man Searching for Purpose

For restless hearts chasing meaning beyond the noise.

Letter 7 – To the Brother Who Refuses to Quit

For the man who keeps standing, even when it hurts.

Letter 8 – To the Husband Learning to Lead with Love

For marriages, learning that leadership begins with humility.

Letter 9 – To the Man Who Feels Forgotten

For the brother waiting in silence, unseen but loved.

Letter 10 – To the Man Who Wants to Leave a Legacy

For every man who longs to finish faithfully and live for eternity.

Closing Sections

1. The Path of Pursuit
2. Prayer for the Reader
3. My Commitment
4. Recommended Scriptures for Continued Growth
5. Themes & Principles Reflected in This Book
6. Final Charge
7. About the Author

✦ DAY 1 – Jesus Defeated Death So You Can Live ✦

Scripture: Romans 6:4 (ESV) – "We were buried therefore with him by baptism into death, so that, just as Christ was raised from the dead … we too might walk in newness of life."

Parable:

A seed fell into the cold earth, covered by darkness and forgotten by the world. Days passed. The soil pressed hard, rain soaked deep, and silence reigned. Yet unseen, a pulse stirred beneath. What seemed like a burial was preparation. When sunlight finally pierced the ground, the seed rose, was recreated, and was no longer what it was, but what it was always meant to be. This parable illustrates how God's timing and unseen work in our lives can transform what seems like a burial into a preparation for a new beginning.

Reflection:

The death of Jesus redefined what endings mean. What the world calls finished, God calls fertile. Every dark place in your life can hold the potential of resurrection. When you surrender to God's timing, you learn that buried things are not lost — they are being planted.

Christ did not rise to prove His power; He rose to prove His enduring love for you. The same power that raised Him now works within you, shaping your heart and calling you into newness of life.

Death no longer ends stories — it launches them.

Faith in Action:

Identify one area in your life that feels dead or hopeless. Ask God to breathe resurrection into it and then function as though He already has.

✦ THE PURSUIT JOURNAL — Day 1 ✦

Use this space to reflect, write, and pray. The Pursuit Journal is designed to help you slow down, listen to God's voice, and allow wisdom to take root in your heart. It's a tool for personal growth and spiritual development.

Scripture That Stood Out:
_____

What I Heard God Say Today:
_____

Where I Saw His Hand at Work:
_____

One Step I will Take to Live This Out:
_____

(Take your time here. Write freely. This is between you and God.)

✦ DAY 2 – I am Nothing Without Jesus ✦

Scripture: John 15:5 (ESV) – "I am the vine; you are the branches. Whoever abides in me and I in him, he it is that bears much fruit, for apart from me you can do nothing."

Parable:

A lamp sat proudly in the center of a room, confident in its glow. When the power was cut, the room fell silent and dark. The lamp realized something essential — the light was not its own. It was borrowed, sustained by connection. Without the current, it was just a shell. When the current returned, the lamp did not boast; it simply shone with gratitude for the power flowing through it.

Reflection:

We live in a culture obsessed with self-sufficiency. But the more profound truth is this: independence from God always leads to burnout. Real strength is not self-made — it is Spirit-supplied.

Jesus calls us to abide, not achieve. Connection, not control, is what bears fruit. When you abide, you are not asking God to power your agenda; you are aligning your heart with His. That is where peace, clarity, and power begin.

When life goes dim, do not change the bulb — check the source.

Faith in Action:

Pause three times today and whisper, "Apart from You, I can do nothing." Watch how that humility transforms your peace and pace.

✦ THE PURSUIT JOURNAL — Day 2 ✦

Use this space to reflect, write, and pray. Let your heart slow down. Wisdom takes root when you stop to listen.

Scripture That Stood Out:
_____

What I Heard God Say Today:
_____

Where I Saw His Hand at Work:
_____

One Step I will Take to Live This Out:
_____

(Take your time here. Write freely. This is between you and God.)

✦ DAY 3 – The Bible Has Wisdom You Might Not Imagine ✦

Scripture: Psalm 119:105 (ESV) – "Your word is a lamp to my feet and a light to my path."

Parable:

A sailor charted his course with the stars until clouds rolled in, covering the sky for weeks. Lost in fog, he drifted until he found an old compass tucked away. The needle pointed steadily north despite the storm. Though he could not see the stars, he realized he did not need to — the compass guided him home.

Reflection:

God's Word is your guiding compass. The Bible does not move with culture; it orients you to Heaven. When every voice around you shouts, "Go this way!" Scripture whispers, "Come this way."

You will never outgrow your need for God's Word. Wisdom is not gained through opinions but through obedience. The Bible does not change to suit you — it changes you to suit truth.

Open it daily, not as a ritual, but as a rescue.

Faith in Action:

Before checking your phone in the morning, read one verse and write it somewhere visible. Carry it through your day like a compass point.

✦ THE PURSUIT JOURNAL — Day 3 ✦

Use this space to reflect, write, and pray. Let your heart slow down. Wisdom takes root when you stop to listen.

Scripture That Stood Out:
_____

What I Heard God Say Today:
_____

Where I Saw His Hand at Work:
_____

One Step I will Take to Live This Out:
_____

(Take your time here. Write freely. This is between you and God.)

✦ DAY 4 – This Too Shall Pass ✦

Scripture: 2 Corinthians 4:17 (ESV) – "For this light momentary affliction is preparing for us an eternal weight of glory beyond all comparison."

Parable:

A storm raged across the mountain, tearing branches, soaking the ground, and bending trees to breaking. When the sun rose, everything dripped with gold. What had looked ruined was radiant. The mountain stood stronger — its roots driven deeper by the very storm that tried to destroy it.

Reflection:

Suffering can feel endless when you are inside it. But eternity rewrites the story. God allows storms not to punish you but to prepare you.

Every trial builds endurance. Every disappointment deepens dependence. What feels like loss is often the foundation of strength. When life shakes, your roots either snap or dig more profoundly — and only surrender determines which.

One day, the storm that once terrified you will become the testimony that strengthens someone else.

Faith in Action:

List one current trial and thank God for what it is teaching you. Gratitude turns pain into purpose.

✦ THE PURSUIT JOURNAL — Day 4 ✦

Use this space to reflect, write, and pray. Let your heart slow down. Wisdom takes root when you stop to listen.

Scripture That Stood Out:
_____

What I Heard God Say Today:
_____

Where I Saw His Hand at Work:
_____

One Step I will Take to Live This Out:
_____

(Take your time here. Write freely. This is between you and God.)

✦ DAY 5 – The Greatest Minds and the Scriptures ✦

Scripture: Proverbs 9:10 (ESV) – "The fear of the Lord is the beginning of wisdom, and the knowledge of the Holy One is insight."

Parable:

A man studied all his life — libraries filled, notebooks covered, degrees framed. Yet peace never visited. One evening, as the sun set across his books, he opened Scripture and read one verse aloud. For the first time, he felt understanding, not from intellect but from reverence. Knowledge filled his head; awe filled his heart. That was the night wisdom began.

Reflection:

Wisdom begins when pride ends. Reverence opens doors intellect never can. The wisest men do not seek applause; they seek alignment.

Learning is a gift, but worship is the doorway to understanding. The Bible reveals not just what is true, but who is truth. When you start with God, everything else finds its place.

Humility is not weakness — it is the posture where wisdom grows.

Faith in Action:

Before starting your work today, pray, "Teach me." Invite God to instruct, not just inform you.

✦ THE PURSUIT JOURNAL — Day 5 ✦

Use this space to reflect, write, and pray. Let your heart slow down. Wisdom takes root when you stop to listen.

Scripture That Stood Out:
_____

What I Heard God Say Today:
_____

Where I Saw His Hand at Work:
_____

One Step I will Take to Live This Out:
_____

(Take your time here. Write freely. This is between you and God.)

✦ DAY 6 – True Progress Requires the Right Destination ✦

Scripture: Proverbs 14:12 (ESV) – "There is a way that seems right to a man, but its end is the way to death."

Parable:

A runner trained for years, pushing harder every day. On race day, he sprinted at full speed — but halfway through, he realized he was on the wrong track. All his effort meant nothing without direction. He slowed, turned around, and ran the right path. Though he finished last, he finished true.

Reflection:

Our culture celebrates speed but ignores direction. God does not measure progress by pace; He measures it by obedience.

Sometimes the bravest thing you can do is stop. Repentance is not failure — it is course correction. When you realign your path with truth, every step becomes progress again.

Do not confuse movement with momentum. God leads with precision, not pressure.

Faith in Action:

Review your goals this week. Cross off one that glorifies you more than God. Replace it with one that builds His Kingdom.

✦ THE PURSUIT JOURNAL — Day 6 ✦

Use this space to reflect, write, and pray. Let your heart slow down. Wisdom takes root when you stop to listen.

Scripture That Stood Out:
_____

What I Heard God Say Today:
_____

Where I Saw His Hand at Work:
_____

One Step I will Take to Live This Out:
_____

(Take your time here. Write freely. This is between you and God.)

✦ DAY 7 – Hope Over Hate ✦

Scripture: Romans 12:21 (ESV) – "Do not be overcome by evil but overcome evil with good."

Parable:

Two fires burned — one of anger, one of grace. The first raged brightly but burned out quickly, leaving only ashes. The second glowed steadily through wind and rain, warming everything nearby. In time, travelers gathered around it, drawn to its light. The fire of grace did not just survive; it saved.

Reflection:

Hate is loud but short-lived. Love lasts because it draws power from eternity. The Spirit of God does not respond to evil with revenge but with redemption.

Every time you choose grace over rage, Heaven wins a battle in you. Hope is not weakness; it is strength under control.

When hate shouts, whisper truth. When bitterness calls, answer with mercy.

Faith in Action:

Reach out to someone who has hurt you or disagrees with you. Pray blessings over them instead of bitterness.

✦ THE PURSUIT JOURNAL — Day 7 ✦

Use this space to reflect, write, and pray. Let your heart slow down. Wisdom takes root when you stop to listen.

Scripture That Stood Out:
_____

What I Heard God Say Today:
_____

Where I Saw His Hand at Work:
_____

One Step I will Take to Live This Out:
_____

(Take your time here. Write freely. This is between you and God.)

✦ DAY 8 – Here I Am, Lord — Send Me ✦

Scripture: Isaiah 6:8 (ESV) – "And I heard the voice of the Lord saying, 'Whom shall I send, and who will go for us?' Then I said, 'Here I am! Send me.'"

Parable:

A young soldier stood at the edge of a vast field. He was not the strongest or the most skilled, but he was willing. As the call echoed across the valley, others hesitated. He stepped forward, trembling but determined. His courage did not come from confidence in himself — it came from trust in the One who called.

Reflection:

God rarely chooses the qualified — He qualifies the chosen. Availability matters more than ability. The man who says, "Here I am," before he knows the assignment is the one God uses to move mountains.

You may not feel ready, but obedience is not about readiness — it is about response. When you say yes to God, He fills the gaps you fear most.

Faith begins at the edge of comfort.

Faith in Action:

Say yes to one thing today that stretches your faith — a conversation, an act of service, or a step of obedience.

✦ THE PURSUIT JOURNAL — Day 8 ✦

Use this space to reflect, write, and pray. Let your heart slow down. Wisdom takes root when you stop to listen.

Scripture That Stood Out:
_____

What I Heard God Say Today:
_____

Where I Saw His Hand at Work:
_____

One Step I will Take to Live This Out:
_____

(Take your time here. Write freely. This is between you and God.)

✦ DAY 9 – Freedom Requires Responsibility ✦

Scripture: Galatians 5:13 (ESV) – "For you were called to freedom, brothers. Only do not use your freedom as an opportunity for the flesh, but through love serve one another."

Parable:

A man tore down a fence around his field to feel free. Soon, weeds crept in, and wandering animals trampled his crops. The wall had not been a prison — it was protection. True freedom was not found in doing anything he wanted; it was found in using his liberty wisely.

Reflection:

Freedom is not the right to do whatever you want — it is the power to do what is right.

God calls us to use our freedom to serve, not to sin. Every choice is stewardship. When we treat grace as permission instead of power, we lose the very freedom Christ died to give.

Responsibility is the fruit of maturity. Freedom without it leads to chaos.

Faith in Action:

Serve someone today without being asked. Freedom grows when love leads.

✦ THE PURSUIT JOURNAL — Day 9 ✦

Use this space to reflect, write, and pray. Let your heart slow down. Wisdom takes root when you stop to listen.

Scripture That Stood Out:
_____

What I Heard God Say Today:
_____

Where I Saw His Hand at Work:
_____

One Step I will Take to Live This Out:
_____

(Take your time here. Write freely. This is between you and God.)

✦ DAY 10 – Grace That Lifts the Fallen ✦

Scripture: Ephesians 2:8 (ESV) – "For by grace you have been saved through faith. And this is not your own doing; it is the gift of God."

Parable:

A potter's vessel collapsed in his hands. Instead of discarding the clay, he gathered it, softened it again, and reshaped it into something more substantial. The marks of failure became the texture of beauty. Grace, like the potter, does not throw away the broken ones; it rebuilds them with purpose.

Reflection:

Grace is not God ignoring sin; it is God redeeming sinners. The same hands that shape galaxies shape your life through mercy.

Failure is never final in the hands of grace. When you fall, God does not fold His arms in disappointment — He extends them in restoration. What disqualifies you in your eyes becomes material for His testimony.

You are the clay; His grace is the fire that refines you.

Faith in Action:

Forgive yourself for something God has already forgiven. Move forward as one shaped, not shamed, by grace.

✦ THE PURSUIT JOURNAL — Day 10 ✦

Use this space to reflect, write, and pray. Let your heart slow down. Wisdom takes root when you stop to listen.

Scripture That Stood Out:
_____

What I Heard God Say Today:
_____

Where I Saw His Hand at Work:
_____

One Step I will Take to Live This Out:
_____

(Take your time here. Write freely. This is between you and God.)

✦ DAY 11 – Identity in Christ ✦

Scripture: 2 Corinthians 5:17 (ESV) – "Therefore, if anyone is in Christ, he is a new creation. The old has passed away; behold, the new has come."

Parable:

A mirror shattered on the ground, reflecting only fragments of faces and light. An artist gathered the broken glass and reassembled it into a mosaic. The reflection was no longer perfect — it was more beautiful. What once revealed flaws now told a story of redemption.

Reflection:

Your identity is not built on what you have done; it is grounded in who God says you are. The world defines you by performance — Jesus defines you by purpose.

In Christ, your past is not your prison. It is proof of what grace can rebuild. You are not the sum of your mistakes — you are the story of His mercy.

Every scar becomes part of His masterpiece.

Faith in Action:

Speak this truth aloud: "I am a new creation in Christ." Let that reality silence every lie that tries to name you.

✦ THE PURSUIT JOURNAL — Day 11 ✦

Use this space to reflect, write, and pray. Let your heart slow down. Wisdom takes root when you stop to listen.

Scripture That Stood Out:
_____

What I Heard God Say Today:
_____

Where I Saw His Hand at Work:
_____

One Step I will Take to Live This Out:
_____

(Take your time here. Write freely. This is between you and God.)

✦ DAY 12 – Gratitude and Humility ✦

Scripture: 1 Thessalonians 5:18 (ESV) – "Give thanks in all circumstances; for this is the will of God in Christ Jesus for you."

Parable:

A mountain stood proud above the valley until fog rolled in and covered its peak. Hidden from view, it no longer drew admiration. Yet the mountain discovered peace — it did not need to be seen to stand strong. Gratitude replaced pride, and humility became its most excellent height.

Reflection:

Being grateful shifts focus from what is missing to what is meaningful. Humility accepts that every blessing is borrowed.

When pride fades, peace enters. The humble heart is not weak; it is wise enough to remember that God is the giver of all good things.

A thankful man is unstoppable — not because life is perfect, but because his joy does not depend on circumstance.

Faith in Action:

Thank God today for something that once frustrated you. Gratitude turns struggle into strength.

✦ THE PURSUIT JOURNAL — Day 12 ✦

Use this space to reflect, write, and pray. Let your heart slow down. Wisdom takes root when you stop to listen.

Scripture That Stood Out:
_____

What I Heard God Say Today:
_____

Where I Saw His Hand at Work:
_____

One Step I will Take to Live This Out:
_____

(Take your time here. Write freely. This is between you and God.)

✦ DAY 13 – Purpose in Every Season ✦

Scripture: Ecclesiastes 3:1 (ESV) – "For everything there is a season, and a time for every matter under heaven."

Parable:

A seed cursed the cold earth of winter until it learned that roots only grow deep when the surface is frozen. When spring came, it did not bloom by accident — it bloomed by endurance.

Reflection:

Every season has purpose — even the quiet ones. God does not rush growth; He refines it.

Waiting is not wasted when God is working beneath the surface. What looks like stillness is soil strengthening your foundation.

If you feel buried, remember — winter always ends.

Faith in Action:

Stop asking "Why this season?" and start asking "What are you teaching me in it?"

✦ THE PURSUIT JOURNAL — Day 13 ✦

Use this space to reflect, write, and pray. Let your heart slow down. Wisdom takes root when you stop to listen.

Scripture That Stood Out:
_____

What I Heard God Say Today:
_____

Where I Saw His Hand at Work:
_____

One Step I will Take to Live This Out:
_____

(Take your time here. Write freely. This is between you and God.)

✦ DAY 14 – Anchored in Truth ✦

Scripture: John 8:32 (ESV) – "And you will know the truth, and the truth will set you free."

Parable:

A ship left harbor on calm seas, its captain certain of fair weather. When a storm hit, panic set in until the anchor dropped. The waves still roared, but the vessel held steady. It was not the size of the ship that saved it — it was the strength of its anchor.

Reflection:

Truth does not change with the tide. When you anchor to Scripture, you do not avoid storms — you outlast them.

Culture drifts: conviction holds. The man who knows truth does not need approval to stand — he needs faith to endure.

Freedom comes not from avoiding storms but from trusting the One who calms them.

Faith in Action:

Memorize one verse this week and anchor your thoughts to it when doubt or temptation strikes.

✦ **THE PURSUIT JOURNAL — Day 14** ✦

Use this space to reflect, write, and pray. Let your heart slow down. Wisdom takes root when you stop to listen.

Scripture That Stood Out:
_____

What I Heard God Say Today:
_____

Where I Saw His Hand at Work:
_____

One Step I will Take to Live This Out:
_____

(Take your time here. Write freely. This is between you and God.)

✦ DAY 15 – We Are Pilgrims, Not Residents ✦

Scripture: Hebrews 13:14 (ESV) – "For here we have no lasting city, but we seek the city that is to come."

Parable:

A traveler stopped at an inn and began hanging pictures, planting flowers, and building fences. When morning came, the road called again. Looking back, he realized how foolish it was to decorate a place he was never meant to stay.

Reflection:

The world is a rest stop, not a residence. God places us here with purpose, not permanence. The moment we mistake temporary comfort for eternal calling, our journey slows.

Live ready to move when God says, "Go." Do not let possessions or status tie you down — the Kingdom ahead is far greater than anything here.

Pilgrims walk lightly because they trust what is leading their steps.

Faith in Action:

Empty your heart, let go of one thing you have been clinging to as if it were forever.

✦ THE PURSUIT JOURNAL — Day 15 ✦

Use this space to reflect, write, and pray. Let your heart slow down. Wisdom takes root when you stop to listen.

Scripture That Stood Out:
_____

What I Heard God Say Today:
_____

Where I Saw His Hand at Work:
_____

One Step I will Take to Live This Out:
_____

(Take your time here. Write freely. This is between you and God.)

✦ DAY 16 – Stay on the Narrow Way ✦

Scripture: Matthew 7:14 (ESV) – "For the gate is narrow and the way is hard that leads to life, and those who find it are few."

Parable:

Two paths stretched through a valley. One was broad, smooth, and crowded with laughter; the other, narrow, rocky, and silent. The traveler paused, uncertain. The wide path promised ease yet felt hollow. The narrow one looked hard, yet something within whispered, "This way." With each careful step, peace replaced comfort, and joy replaced applause. At journey's end, he found life where few dared to walk.

Reflection:

The narrow path is not popular, but it is purposeful. Following Christ has always meant swimming against the current — not out of rebellion, but obedience. The road that leads to life will assess your faith, stretch your convictions, and refine your motives.

God's way is rarely easy, but it is always worth it. What the world calls restrictive, Heaven calls redemptive. When you stay on the narrow path, you find more than survival — you see the Savior walking beside you.

Every step that costs you something will be rewarded by someone greater.

Faith in Action:

When you face a moral shortcut today, take the narrow route. Obedience rarely comes easily, but it always pays off.

✦ THE PURSUIT JOURNAL — Day 16 ✦

Use this space to reflect, write, and listen. Wisdom grows when your spirit slows.

Scripture That Stood Out:
_____

What I Heard God Say Today:
_____

Where I Saw His Hand at Work:
_____

One Step I will Take to Walk the Narrow Way:
_____

(Take your time here. Let truth settle in your soul before you move on.)

✦ DAY 17 – Scripture Ahead of Its Time

Scripture: Isaiah 40:8 (ESV) – "The grass withers, the flower fades, but the word of our God will stand forever."

Parable:

Empires rose and fell, philosophies shifted, and languages died — yet one book remained. Burned, banned, and buried, still it lived. The Bible outlasted kings, critics, and centuries. Every attempt to silence it only spreads it further. It does not merely survive time; it defines it. Truth does not grow old — it grows proven.

Reflection:

The Word of God is not a trend — it is a foundation. What was written in ancient times still speaks with power because truth is timeless. God's Word does not echo; it declares.

Every generation tries to improve or ignore Scripture, yet it stands unshaken. The same Word that guided Abraham guides you. Every promise written still holds its pulse.

When you open your Bible, you are not reading history; you are hearing eternity whisper hope into the present.

Faith in Action:

Read a familiar verse today as if you have never seen it before. Ask God to breathe new light into old truth.

✦ THE PURSUIT JOURNAL — Day 17 ✦

Use this space to reflect, write, and listen. Wisdom grows when your spirit slows.

Scripture That Stood Out:
_____

What I Heard God Say Today:
_____

Where I Saw His Hand at Work:
_____

One Step I will Take to Treasure His Word:
_____

(Take your time here. Let the Word speak before you do.)

✦ DAY 18 – We All Fall Short ✦

Scripture: Romans 3:23 (ESV) – "For all have sinned and fall short of the glory of God."

Parable:

A mountain climber lost his grip and fell. Hanging by a fraying rope, he expected condemnation but heard a voice say, "Hold on." A strong hand reached down, lifted him, and steadied him again. The rescuer smiled and said, "You are not done climbing. You are just learning to trust."

Reflection:

Falling does not end faith — quitting does. Every stumble can become a lesson if you let grace teach instead of guilt torment.

Sin reveals our need for a Savior. God's response to our failure is not rejection; it is redemption. The enemy wants you to believe you are disqualified; God says, "You're still mine."

When you fall, fall toward Him. Mercy does not erase mistakes — it restores momentum.

Faith in Action:

Confess one area of struggle today, not from shame but with expectation. Grace is already waiting at the bottom of your fall.

✦ THE PURSUIT JOURNAL — Day 18 ✦

Use this space to reflect, write, and listen. Wisdom grows when your spirit slows.

Scripture That Stood Out:
_____

What I Heard God Say Today:
_____

Where I Saw His Hand at Work:
_____

One Step I will Take to Live Redeemed:
_____

(Take your time here. Let grace rewrite your reflection.)

✦ DAY 19 – Conviction Is Contagious ✦

Scripture: 1 Corinthians 16:13 (ESV) – "Be watchful, stand firm in the faith, act like men, be strong."

Parable:

In a dark valley, one torch flickered alone. Winds blew, rain fell, but the flame endured. A passerby saw it and lit his own. Soon, dozens glowed. The valley did not brighten all at once — it brightened because one refused to go out.

Reflection:

Conviction is not loud; it is steady. The world does not need more noise — it needs men who quietly burn with truth.

Faithfulness inspires far beyond what you will ever see. Every stand for righteousness sparks another. When you hold the line, others find the courage to join you.

Let your convictions be so rooted in Christ that culture cannot shake them and fear cannot quench them.

Faith in Action:

Do one small thing today that reflects conviction — not comfort. Your consistency is your witness.

✦ THE PURSUIT JOURNAL — Day 19 ✦

Use this space to reflect, write, and listen. Wisdom grows when your spirit slows.

Scripture That Stood Out:
_____

What I Heard God Say Today:
_____

Where I Saw His Hand at Work:
_____

One Step I will Take to Live with Conviction:
_____

(Take your time here. Light spreads when you tend your own flame.)

✦ DAY 20 – Defiant Hope ✦

Scripture: Romans 15:13 (ESV) – "May the God of hope fill you with all joy and peace in believing."

Parable:

Night mocked the horizon, certain that light had died. Hours passed, and darkness grew thicker. Yet somewhere beyond sight, the sun began to rise. It did not hurry — it simply came. The night's laughter faded in silence as dawn painted the sky with promise.

Reflection:

Hope is not passive; it is defiant. It looks at chaos and still believes in victory. Sincere hope is not denial of pain — it is defiance of despair.

When you cannot see light, remember that God never sleeps. Even silence is a strategy. Every sunrise preaches resurrection.

Hope does not always roar. Sometimes it whispers, "Keep standing."

Faith in Action:

Reach out to encourage someone who is losing faith. Remind them — morning always comes.

✦ **THE PURSUIT JOURNAL — Day 20** ✦

Use this space to reflect, write, and listen. Wisdom grows when your spirit slows.

Scripture That Stood Out:
_____

What I Heard God Say Today:
_____

Where I Saw His Hand at Work:
_____

One Step I will Take to Choose hope:
_____

(Take your time here. Let hope speak louder than fear.)

✦ DAY 21 – Lessons in Every Season ✦

Scripture: James 1:2–4 (ESV) – "Count it all joy, my brothers, when you meet trials of various kinds, for you know that the testing of your faith produces steadfastness."

Parable:

A river carved its path through rock, not by force but by persistence. For years, it flowed over the same stone until the canyon stood as a monument to patience. It did not rush — it remained.

Reflection:

Growth takes time, and time takes trust. God uses repetition to shape resilience. What feels like a delay is often divine development.

Joy in trials is not denial — it is recognition that pain produces depth. Faith that has never been assessed remains shallow. But when your endurance is stretched, your roots reach heavenward.

God is not just doing something around you; He is forming something within you.

Faith in Action:

Embrace one frustration today as training, not punishment. Growth and grace share the same classroom.

✦ THE PURSUIT JOURNAL — Day 21 ✦

Use this space to reflect, write, and listen. Wisdom grows when your spirit slows.

Scripture That Stood Out:
_____

What I Heard God Say Today:
_____

Where I Saw His Hand at Work:
_____

One Step I will Take to Learn in This Season:
_____

(Take your time here. Endurance is built in stillness and surrender.)

✦ DAY 22 – The Power of Quiet Strength ✦

Scripture: Proverbs 17:27 (ESV) – "Whoever restrains his words has knowledge, and he who has a cool spirit is a man of understanding."

Parable:

In a crowded room, everyone shouted to be heard. One man listened. When he finally spoke, silence fell — not because he was loud, but because his words carried weight. His restraint was strength, his patience, power.

Reflection:

The loudest voice is not always the strongest. Real strength is steady, not showy. Godly men learn to master their emotions rather than be mastered by them.

A calm spirit reveals confidence in God's control. When you trust Him, you do not need to prove yourself — your peace becomes your defense.

The world craves reaction, Heaven values restraint. Quiet courage will always outlast noisy pride.

Faith in Action:

Pause before speaking today. Let your silence invite wisdom before your words deliver it.

✦ THE PURSUIT JOURNAL — Day 22 ✦

Use this space to reflect, write, and listen. Wisdom grows when your spirit slows.

Scripture That Stood Out:
_____

What I Heard God Say Today:
_____

Where I Saw His Hand at Work:
_____

One Step I will Take Toward Quiet Strength:
_____

(Take your time here. Let stillness speak before sound.)

✦ DAY 23 – Forgiven to Forgive ✦

Scripture: Ephesians 4:32 (ESV) – "Be kind to one another, tenderhearted, forgiving one another, as God in Christ forgave you."

Parable:

A man carried a heavy bag of stones — each one engraved with a name, a wound, or a memory. The weight bent his back and slowed his steps. One day, he knelt and laid them down. In their place, flowers of freedom grew.

Reflection:

Unforgiveness chains the heart more than the offender. God calls us to release not because they deserve it, but because you were first released.

Forgiveness does not erase the wrong; it ends the reign of bitterness. Every act of mercy mirrors the Cross — undeserved but unstoppable.

You cannot walk forward while dragging the past.

Faith in Action:

Write down one name you need to forgive. Pray over it, then tear the paper. Let God hold what you have carried.

✦ THE PURSUIT JOURNAL — Day 23 ✦

Use this space to reflect, write, and listen. Wisdom grows when your spirit slows.

Scripture That Stood Out:
_____

What I Heard God Say Today:
_____

Where I Saw His Hand at Work:
_____

One Step I will Take to Forgive:
_____

(Take your time here. Mercy multiplies in motion.)

✦ DAY 24 – The Strength of Servanthood✦

Scripture: Mark 10:45 (ESV) – "For even the Son of Man came not to be served but to serve, and to give his life as a ransom for many."

Parable:

A king disguised himself as a servant and entered the streets of his city. He listened to his people, carried their burdens, and washed their feet. When he revealed his true identity, they wept — not from fear, but love. They followed him, not because of his crown, but because of his compassion.

Reflection:

Authentic leadership begins with humility. Serving others does not lower you; it lifts everyone around you.

Jesus redefined greatness. His power was not shown in dominance, but in devotion. Every act of service breaks pride's grip and strengthens Christlike character.

You do not serve to be seen — you serve to be shaped.

Faith in Action:

Do one unseen act of service today. Let obedience, not recognition, be your reward.

✦ THE PURSUIT JOURNAL — Day 24 ✦

Use this space to reflect, write, and listen. Wisdom grows when your spirit slows.

Scripture That Stood Out:
_____

What I Heard God Say Today:
_____

Where I Saw His Hand at Work:
_____

One Step I will Take to Serve Boldly:
_____

(Take your time here. The most incredible crowns begin with a towel.)

✦ DAY 25 – Guard Your Mind ✦

Scripture: Romans 12:2 (ESV) – "Do not be conformed to this world but be transformed by the renewal of your mind."

Parable:

A garden left untended grows wild. Weeds choke flowers, vines creep over walls, and beauty fades into chaos. But a gardener who returns daily — pruning, planting, watering — restores order. So, it is with the mind.

Reflection:

Your thoughts are seeds that shape your future. When you fill your mind with truth, you build a fortress of peace. When you neglect it, lies take root.

The battle for holiness begins in the head. God does not just want your actions to change — He wants your perspective transformed.

Feed your mind with Scripture, not fear. Renewal is repetition — one thought at a time.

Faith in Action:

Replace one negative thought with a verse of truth every time it appears. Watch your garden grow clean.

✦ THE PURSUIT JOURNAL — Day 25 ✦

Use this space to reflect, write, and listen. Wisdom grows when your spirit slows.

Scripture That Stood Out:
_____

What I Heard God Say Today:
_____

Where I Saw His Hand at Work:
_____

One Step I will Take to Renew My Mind:
_____

(Take your time here. What you think shapes who you become.)

✦ DAY 26 – Faith That Moves Mountains✦

Scripture: Matthew 17:20 (ESV) – "If you have faith like a grain of mustard seed … nothing will be impossible for you."

Parable:

A boy stared at a mountain blocking his view. He prayed not for it to vanish, but for the strength to climb. Step by step, faith grew stronger than the peak. At the summit, he realized the miracle was not the mountain moving — it was his courage that had.

Reflection:

Faith is not fantasy; it is focus. God does not call us to wish, but to walk.

Sometimes faith moves obstacles; sometimes it moves you. The size of your faith does not matter — the size of your God does.

When you believe, you stop measuring the mountain and start trusting the Maker.

Faith in Action:

Write down one "impossible" thing and pray daily, not for removal, but for readiness.

✦ **THE PURSUIT JOURNAL — Day 26** ✦

Use this space to reflect, write, and listen. Wisdom grows when your spirit slows.

Scripture That Stood Out:
_____

What I Heard God Say Today:
_____

Where I Saw His Hand at Work:
_____

One Step I will Take to Walk in Faith:
_____

(Take your time here. Faith grows in motion.)

✦ DAY 27 – Courage in the Fire ✦

Scripture: Daniel 3:17–18 (ESV) – "Our God whom we serve is able to deliver us … but if not, be it known to you, O king, that we will not serve your gods."

Parable:

Three men stood before the fire — not because of rebellion, but conviction. Flames roared, guards mocked, yet their faith did not flinch. They were not saved from the fire, but through it — and the fourth man walked with them.

Reflection:

Courage isn't not being afraid; it is the presence of faith that refuses to bow. God may not consistently deliver you from the trial, but He will always meet you in it.

The fire that threatens to destroy can become the place where His glory shines brightest.

Stand firm. Even if.

Faith in Action:

Face one fear today by standing for truth instead of comfort. Your faith is stronger than the flames.

✦ THE PURSUIT JOURNAL — Day 27 ✦

Use this space to reflect, write, and listen. Wisdom grows when your spirit slows.

Scripture That Stood Out:
_____

What I Heard God Say Today:
_____

Where I Saw His Hand at Work:
_____

One Step I will Take to Stand Courageously:
_____

(Take your time here. Fire reveals faith, not failure.)

✦ DAY 28 – The Power of God's Word ✦

Scripture: Hebrews 4:12 (ESV) – "For the word of God is living and active, sharper than any two-edged sword."

Parable:

A soldier entered battle with nothing but himself and the Word. His enemies mocked until they realized that every lie that came against him fell silent when truth was spoken. Victory came not through strength, but through Scripture.

Reflection:

The Bible is not a relic; it is a weapon. It cuts lies, heals hearts, and reveals motives.

When you speak God's Word, you wield His authority. Satan does not fear opinions — he fears Scripture spoken with belief.

Sharpen your sword daily. The Word defends, directs, and delivers.

Faith in Action:

Take the time to memorize one verse that speaks to your current situation. Use it when fear or doubt attacks.

✦ **THE PURSUIT JOURNAL — Day 28** ✦

Use this space to reflect, write, and listen. Wisdom grows when your spirit slows.

Scripture That Stood Out:
_____

What I Heard God Say Today:
_____

Where I Saw His Hand at Work:
_____

One Step I will Take to Wield His Word:
_____

(Take your time here. The sharpest sword is Scripture, believed.)

✦ DAY 29 – Faith Over Fear ✦

Scripture: Joshua 1:9 (ESV) – "Be strong and courageous. Do not be frightened, and do not be dismayed, for the Lord your God is with you wherever you go."

Parable:

A boy stepped into deep water for the first time. Fear shouted, "You'll sink!" But his father's voice said, "I've got you." He took one trembling step, then another — until he was floating, carried by trust.

Reflection:

Fear whispers doubt where faith declares truth. Courage is not the absence of fear; it is choosing trust in the face of it.

When you remember who walks with you, every "what if" loses power, the presence of God does not eliminate fear — it eclipses it.

Faith and fear both ask you to believe something that has not happened yet. Choose faith.

Faith in Action:

When anxiety strikes today, pause and speak: "God is with me." Repeat until fear fades.

✦ **THE PURSUIT JOURNAL — Day 29** ✦

Use this space to reflect, write, and listen. Wisdom grows when your spirit slows.

Scripture That Stood Out:
_____

What I Heard God Say Today:
_____

Where I Saw His Hand at Work:
_____

One Step I will Take to Walk in Faith:
_____

(Take your time here. Fear flees when faith speaks.)

✦ DAY 30 – Finish the Race ✦

Scripture: 2 Timothy 4:7 (ESV) – "I have fought the good fight, I have finished the race, I have kept the faith."

Parable:

A runner stumbled seven times, scared and weary. Others passed, but he rose repeatedly. At the finish line, his steps were slow, but his eyes never left the goal. When he crossed, Heaven stood.

Reflection:

Faithfulness is not about speed — it is about endurance. God does not call you to win; He calls you to finish. Every failure forgiven, every tear seen, every struggle recorded in grace.

You do not run alone. The One who began your race runs beside you until the end.

Keep going. Heaven is closer than you think.

Faith in Action:

Reflect on how far God has brought you. Then take one more step forward. The finish line is faithfulness.

✦ **THE PURSUIT JOURNAL — Day 30** ✦

Use this space to reflect, write, and listen. Wisdom grows when your spirit slows.

Scripture That Stood Out:
_____

What I Heard God Say Today:
_____

Where I Saw His Hand at Work:
_____

One Step I will Take to Finish Well:
_____

(Take your time here. The finish line is closer than you think.)

✦ **7 Bonus Days– The Pursuit Continues**✦

✦ DAY 31 – The Pursuit Continues ✦

Scripture: Philippians 3:14 (ESV) – "I press on toward the goal for the prize of the upward call of God in Christ Jesus."

Parable:

A blacksmith hammered steel until sparks filled the room. Each strike shaped, each flame refined. The blade was not made in comfort but through consistent pressure. When cooled, it gleamed — not because the fire destroyed it, but because it defined it.

Reflection:

Faith is not a moment — it is a pursuit. Growth in God happens when you stay in the forge of formation. The heat you endure is not punishment; it is preparation.

God does not stop working when you are weary; He strengthens you through it. The call upward is lifelong. Do not stop when you are tired — stop when you're transformed.

Faith in Action:

Write down one area where you've seen God's growth through struggle. Thank Him for the fire that forged your strength.

✦ THE PURSUIT JOURNAL — Day 31 ✦

Use this space to reflect, write, and listen. Wisdom grows when your spirit slows.

Scripture That Stood Out:
_____

What I Heard God Say Today:
_____

Where I Saw His Hand at Work:
_____

One Step I'll Take to Keep Pursuing:
_____

(Take your time here. Growth takes endurance.)

✦ DAY 32 – A Man of Integrity ✦

Scripture: Proverbs 10:9 (ESV) – "Whoever walks in integrity walks securely, but he who makes his ways crooked will be found out."

Parable:

A bridge built of rotting wood looked strong until the first storm came. Beneath the paint, decay had been ignored. The collapse was sudden, but the compromise was slow. The builder learned that a hidden weakness always reveals itself under pressure.

Reflection:

Integrity is who you are when no one's watching. It's the daily choice to honor God in the unseen.

The world rewards appearance; God rewards authenticity. When you walk upright, your footing stays firm, even when storms rage.

Integrity is security — not because it's easy, but because it's anchored in truth.

Faith in Action:

Examine one undisclosed area of your life. Align it with God's truth before a storm does it for you.

✦ THE PURSUIT JOURNAL — Day 32 ✦

Use this space to reflect, write, and listen.

Scripture That Stood Out:

_____

What I Heard God Say Today:

_____

Where I Saw His Hand at Work:

_____

One Step I'll Take Toward Integrity:

_____

(Take your time here. Wholeness brings peace.)

✦ DAY 33 – The Battle Within ✦

Scripture: Galatians 5:17 (ESV) – "For the desires of the flesh are against the Spirit, and the desires of the Spirit are against the flesh."

Parable:

Inside a warrior's heart, two wolves fought — one of pride, the other of purity. Each day, only one grew stronger. The difference wasn't strength or skill — it was which one he fed.

Reflection:

Every man lives with tension between flesh and spirit. The one you feed will rule.

Discipline isn't about perfection; it's about choosing which voice wins. The spirit leads to freedom; the flesh leads to frustration.

You are not defined by your desires but by your decisions.

Faith in Action:

Fast one thing today that feeds the flesh and replace it with something that feeds your faith.

✦ THE PURSUIT JOURNAL — Day 33 ✦

Use this space to reflect, write, and listen.

Scripture That Stood Out:
_____

What I Heard God Say Today:
_____

Where I Saw His Hand at Work:
_____

One Step I'll Take to Win the Battle Within:
_____

(Take your time here. Victory begins with awareness.)

✦ DAY 34 – Purpose Over Pleasure ✦

Scripture: Psalm 16:11 (ESV) – "You make known to me the path of life; in your presence there is fullness of joy; at your right hand are pleasures forevermore."

Parable:

A man chased shadows, each one promising joy. Every time he reached them, they vanished. One day, he stopped, turned, and found the sun behind him — the source of the light he'd been chasing.

Reflection:

Pleasure fades when it's the goal; purpose fulfills when it's the guide. God's presence satisfies more deeply than any earthly thrill.

The pursuit of holiness isn't about denying joy — it's about finding it in the right place. You don't have to chase shadows when you walk in the light.

Choose purpose. Pleasure will follow.

Faith in Action:

Trade one indulgence today for intentional time in God's presence. Joy will meet you there.

✦ THE PURSUIT JOURNAL — Day 34 ✦

Use this space to reflect, write, and listen.

Scripture That Stood Out:
_____

What I Heard God Say Today:
_____

Where I Saw His Hand at Work:
_____

One Step I'll Take Toward Purpose:
_____

(Take your time here. Lasting joy lives in presence, not pleasure.)

✦ DAY 35 – Faith That Endures ✦

Scripture: Hebrews 10:36 (ESV) – "For you have need of endurance, so that when you have done the will of God you may receive what is promised."

Parable:

A candle burned low after long hours, its flame flickering. The keeper didn't snuff it out — he shielded it until it steadied again. The smallest flame, protected, still brings light through the longest night.

Reflection:

Endurance is faith's second wind. It's not about never faltering but never quitting.

When you want to give up, remember — God finishes what He starts. The promise hasn't failed; it's forming.

Steady faith shines brightly when everything else fades.

Faith in Action:

Refuse to quit today — on prayer, on progress, on purpose. Hold steady. The promise is near.

✦ THE PURSUIT JOURNAL — Day 35 ✦

Use this space to reflect, write, and listen.

Scripture That Stood Out:
_____

What I Heard God Say Today:
_____

Where I Saw His Hand at Work:
_____

One Step I'll Take to Endure in Faith:
_____

(Take your time here. Even a flicker can defeat the dark.)

✦ DAY 36 – God's Timing Is Perfect ✦

Scripture: Ecclesiastes 3:11 (ESV) – "He has made everything beautiful in its time."

Parable:

A watchmaker built a masterpiece, every gear precise. The impatient apprentice tried to rush the process, breaking the balance. Only when time was restored did the watch keep perfect rhythm again.

Reflection:

God's timing doesn't match our clocks. Impatience breaks what trust would build.

What you see as delay, God sees as design. The waiting seasons are not wasted — they prepare you for what's next.

When you surrender control of when, you'll discover peace in who.

Faith in Action:

Stop asking "When, God?" and start saying "I trust You." Rest is worship in motion.

✦ **THE PURSUIT JOURNAL — Day 36** ✦

Use this space to reflect, write, and listen.

Scripture That Stood Out:
_____

What I Heard God Say Today:
_____

Where I Saw His Hand at Work:
_____

One Step I'll Take to Trust His Timing:
_____

(Take your time here. Time isn't wasted when it's surrendered.)

✦ DAY 37 – A Life Worth Remembering

Scripture: Matthew 25:23 (ESV) – "Well done, good and faithful servant."

Parable:

A craftsman finished his final work — not the grandest piece, but the truest. When asked what made it great, he said, "Every cut was for the Master's pleasure." His reward wasn't fame — it was the Master's smile.

Reflection:

Legacy isn't about being remembered by many; it's about being recognized by One. A life well-lived point beyond itself.

Faithfulness in the small leads to fruitfulness in the eternal. When your story ends, may Heaven stand because you served well on earth.

Faith in Action:

Do something today that no one will thank you for — but Heaven will notice.

✦ THE PURSUIT JOURNAL — Day 37 ✦

Use this space to reflect, write, and listen.

Scripture That Stood Out:
_____

What I Heard God Say Today:
_____

Where I Saw His Hand at Work:
_____

One Step I'll Take to Build Legacy:
_____

(Take your time here. The Master's "well done" is worth every step.)

✦ LETTERS TO MY BROTHERS ✦

(A Word from My Heart to Yours)

Letter 1 – To the Man Who's Just Beginning

Brother, don't let fear whisper that it's too late for you to start, or that you need to have everything figured out before you walk with God. Every mighty man of faith began right where you are — unsure, imperfect, but willing. Noah built before it rained. Abraham obeyed before he knew where to go. Peter dropped his net before he understood who Jesus really was.

You don't have to know the whole map — trust the One holding it. Every step of obedience is another stone in the foundation of a life built on faith. There will be days you'll fall short, and nights you'll wonder if you're even cut out for this. That's okay. God's not looking for perfection; He's looking for persistence.

You'll learn more in the stumble than you ever could in safety. Every scar will tell a story of His mercy. Keep opening your Bible when it feels dry. Keep praying when Heaven feels quiet. Keep showing up when nobody else does.

Starting small doesn't mean staying small. The same God who called fishermen and farmers is calling you. Don't overcomplicate it — begin. The rest will unfold in His timing.

Letter 2 – To the Husband Who Feels Tired

Brother, I see you. You carry more than you talk about — the bills, the expectations, the quiet pressure to keep it all together. Some days it feels like everyone's leaning on you while you're running on fumes. You're not weak for being weary; you're human.

Marriage was never meant to be effortless — it's meant to be eternal. Love isn't measured in butterflies but in battle scars. Some nights you'll go to bed frustrated, feeling unseen or unappreciated. But don't let that lie steal your resolve. God honors the husband who stays when it would be easier to run, who prays when it would be easier to argue.

Remember this: your leadership doesn't come from domination; it comes from devotion. When you serve your wife, you reflect Christ washing feet — not a king demanding a throne. Lead with tenderness. Pursue her heart even when she seems distant. Choose patience when your pride wants to speak first.

There's more at stake than your comfort — your marriage is a picture of the Gospel. Keep loving her like Christ loved the church: sacrificially, consistently, even when it hurts. God sees you, even if she doesn't right now. Your quiet endurance is holy work.

Letter 3 – To the Father Raising Warriors

Your sons don't need a superhero; they need a real father. They're not looking for flawless — they're looking for faithfulness.

Every boy watches his dad to learn how to be a man — not just in what you say, but in what you do when no one's watching. They're learning how to oversee anger, how to love a woman, how to face failure, and how to talk to God — by watching you.

The world will teach them noise and numbness; you get to teach them presence and prayer. Don't just tell them to be strong — show them how to kneel first. Take them fishing, build something with your hands, pray with them at night. And when you mess up — and you will — let them see repentance too.

You're raising men who will either imitate your faith or heal from your absence. Be the kind of father who makes it easy to believe in the love of the Heavenly One.

Letter 4 – To the Father Raising Daughters

Brother, I know the weight of it — that mix of tenderness and responsibility that comes with raising a daughter. She's watching your every move, learning how men love by how you treat her mother, how you listen, and how you lead.

You're shaping her standard. Your words will echo long after she's grown. Tell her she's beautiful but remind her that beauty fades and character endures. Teach her that strength and grace aren't opposites — they're inseparable.

Don't just protect her body — protect her heart. Remind her often that her worth was decided at the Cross, not in a mirror or a man's opinion. Be her refuge in the chaos of a noisy world.

You won't always get it right. You'll lose your temper, or miss a recital, or misunderstand her tears. But keep showing up. That's what matters. Someday, when a man asks for her hand, she'll remember the first one who held it — and she'll know what to look for.

Letter 5 – To the Man Fighting Quiet Battles

Brother, I know you're tired. You smile in public, but there's a war in your mind no one else sees. You wake up heavy, carry it all day, and collapse into bed, hoping tomorrow will feel lighter.

You're not broken — you're battling. And God hasn't forgotten you. The enemy wants you to be isolated because light exposes lies. Bring your struggle to trusted brothers, to Scripture, to prayer. Confession is not surrendering its strategy.

You can't win what you won't face. But you're not fighting alone. God hasn't just called you to survive — He's called you to overcome. He's still authoring your story, even when you can't see the following line.

Brother, if all you do today is stand — that's victory. If all you can do is whisper a prayer — that's warfare. Keep going. You're not finished; you're being refined.

Letter 6 – To the Young Man Searching for Purpose

You've got fire in your bones and a thousand voices telling you where to spend it. Every ad, every influencer, every crowd says, "Be more. Get more. Prove yourself." But purpose doesn't come from applause — it comes from alignment.

Brother, the call on your life won't always look glamorous. It might look like serving when no one's watching, obeying when it's inconvenient, and saying no when it costs you everything. That's where true men are forged.

Stop comparing your first chapter to someone else's highlight reel. God's timing is not your delay — it's your development. Be faithful in the ordinary. Clean the nets before you fish the seas.

One day, you'll look back and realize every quiet season was a training ground for influence you couldn't manage yet—Chase purpose, not platform. Influence fades; impact lasts.

Letter 7 – To the Brother Who Refuses to Quit

Brother, if you're reading this, it means you're still standing — and that's something Heaven celebrates. The world praises success, but Heaven applauds endurance.

There are moments when faith wants to drag a heavy cross uphill, and you wonder if it's even worth it. It is. Every tear, every unanswered prayer, every act of faith in the dark is seen by God.

You might not see progress, but you're building spiritual muscle that only grows under resistance. The testing of your faith is producing endurance — and endurance produces maturity. (James 1:2–4)

Keep pressing on. Even when you can't run, crawl toward hope. Even when you can't see the finish line, please keep your eyes on the One who already crossed it. You're not losing — you're lasting.

Letter 8 – To the Husband Learning to Lead with Love

Leadership isn't about control — it's about compassion. Jesus led by serving, by listening, by washing feet. You don't have to be loud to lead; you must love first.

You'll make mistakes — we all do. You'll say the wrong thing, you'll fail to notice her pain, and you'll forget that your words carry weight. But humility repairs what pride destroys. Say "I'm sorry" faster. Pray for her when she's quiet. Let your gentleness be strength wrapped in grace.

Authentic leadership begins on your knees. You can't love your wife well until you've learned to let God love you first. Let your leadership be so Christlike that she sees Heaven's reflection in your home.

You're not called to win arguments — you're called to win her heart daily. That's how kings become servants, and servants become like Christ.

Letter 9 – To the Man Who Feels Forgotten

Brother, I know what it feels like to do everything right and still feel invisible. You give your best at work, at home, at church — and no one says thank you. You pray for breakthroughs that do not come. You watch others get what you've been asking for.

But the silence of God isn't the absence of God. He hides those He's shaping. David learned to fight lions in the field before he faced Goliath. Joseph's faith grew in prison before he ever reached the palace.

Hidden seasons are holy seasons. They strip pride and teach you to worship without applause. You don't need to be seen by everyone — just by the One who matters.

Keep tending your sheep. Keep showing up. God is building depth in the dark so that when the light comes, you'll be ready to carry it.

Letter 10 – To the Man Who Wants to Leave a Legacy

Legacy isn't about how many people know your name — it's about how many people know Christ because of you.

Every time you choose faith over fear, truth over comfort, and obedience over convenience, you're laying bricks that will outlast you. Your children may not remember every word you say, but they'll remember your consistency, your compassion, your courage.

You don't have to be famous to be faithful. God doesn't measure success by headlines but by obedience. The world builds monuments to itself; the Kingdom builds men who point to Him.

Brother, one day your race will end. Make sure the footprints you leave behind lead others straight to Jesus. Live so that Heaven knows your name — not because of what you did, but because of who you served.

✦ THE PATH OF PURSUIT ✦

The end of this devotional isn't the end of your journey — it's the beginning of a lifestyle. Pursuing wisdom and godliness doesn't end after 37 days. It continues in how you lead, serve, forgive, and love daily.

The path of pursuit is a road of daily surrender. It's a call to walk humbly before God and boldly before men. Some days will feel like victory; others, like wilderness. Both matters.

When the fire fades and the noise of the world grows louder, return to these truths:

1. Wisdom starts with reverence, not intellect.
2. Godliness thrives in humility, not perfection.
3. True strength is found in surrender, not control.
4. Hope always wins — even when silence lingers.

This isn't just a book to finish — it's a rhythm to live. Keep walking. Keep seeking. Keep becoming.

"The fear of the Lord is the beginning of wisdom." – Proverbs 9:10

✦ PRAYER FOR THE READER ✦

Father,

Thank you to every man who has walked through these pages.

Please give him a spirit of endurance when life grows heavy, courage when conviction costs, and peace that silences fear.

Let Your Word burn brighter than the world's noise. Make his hands strong for service, his heart soft for compassion, and his feet steady in faith.

May he lead with humility, love with strength, and live with eternal vision.

Amen.

✦ MY COMMITMENT ✦

I commit to being a man who pursues wisdom, even when it costs convenience.

I commit to seeking godliness, even when culture offers shortcuts.

I commit to stand firm in truth, lead with love, and live for eternity.

This is not perfection — it's pursuit.

Not arrival — but direction.

Not applause — but obedience.

Signature: _____

Date: _____

✦ RECOMMENDED SCRIPTURES FOR CONTINUED GROWTH ✦

These verses will strengthen your daily walk beyond this devotional. Use them for study, prayer, or journaling as you continue pursuing wisdom and godliness:

1. Proverbs 3:5–6 – Trust in the Lord with all your heart.
2. James 1:5 – If any of you lacks wisdom, let him ask God.
3. Micah 6:8 – Walk humbly with your God.
4. Philippians 4:13 – I can do all things through Christ who strengthens me.
5. Psalm 1:1–3 – Blessed is the man who delights in the law of the Lord.
6. 1 Corinthians 16:13 – Be watchful, stand firm in the faith.
7. Isaiah 40:31 – Those who wait for the Lord shall renew their strength.
8. Romans 12:2 – Be transformed by the renewal of your mind.
9. Matthew 5:16 – Let your light shine before others.
10. 2 Timothy 4:7 – I have fought the good fight; I have finished the race.

✦ THEMES & PRINCIPLES REFLECTED IN THIS BOOK ✦

1. **Wisdom Over Emotion:**
2. True discernment comes from Scripture, not circumstance.
3. **Courage in Conviction:**
4. Strength is revealed not in noise but in steadfast faith.
5. **Grace That Restores:**
6. God's mercy isn't earned; it's embraced.
7. **Purpose Through Pain:**
8. Every trial is preparation. Growth is often hidden under struggle.
9. **Integrity as Identity:**
10. Who you are when unseen matters more than what you display.
11. **Hope as Resistance:**
12. Hope is not denial of hardship but defiance against despair.
13. **Faith That Acts:**
14. Belief without obedience is theory — faith steps forward.
15. **Servanthood as Strength:**
16. The most powerful men are those who kneel first.
17. **Endurance in the Everyday:**
18. God builds greatness in consistency, not applause.
19. **Eternal Perspective:**
20. You're not living for this world — you're training for the next.

✦ FINAL CHARGE ✦

Brother,

You have walked through 37 days of challenge, reflection, and renewal. The pursuit doesn't end here. You have been called to stand firm in a world that drifts, to lead with integrity in a culture of compromise, and to burn with truth when many flicker out.

Don't let this book close without action. Go live what you've learned. The next generation needs your example, your courage, and your conviction.

You were made for this pursuit.

"He who began a good work in you will bring it to completion at the day of Jesus Christ." – Philippians 1:6

✦ ABOUT THE AUTHOR ✦

Marty Bergey is a lover of Jesus, husband, and father of seven.

A former enlisted U.S. Marine and U.S. Army officer, Marty carries the heart of a warrior and strives for the humility of a disciple. He is enthusiastic about discipling and mentoring the next generation of godly men who lead with faith, courage, and integrity.

As an entrepreneur and CEO of Carpe Diem Glazing, Marty is dedicated to Christ in the marketplace and building strong relationships—serving alongside his brother in Christ and business partner, Zachary Snyder.

When he's not leading or teaching, you'll find him outdoors—fishing, hunting, or making memories with his family.

Marty also shares faith, life lessons, and outdoor adventures on his YouTube and TikTok platforms: Fishing the Country.

✦ SCRIPTURE INDEX ✦

(All Scripture quotations are from the English Standard Version – ESV)

A Word Before You Begin

Every page of this book points back to the same source — the living Word of God.

This index is here to guide you deeper into that Word, not just to re-read a verse, but to remember what it stirred in you.

Take time to revisit these Scriptures slowly. Read them aloud. Pray them back to God.

Let His voice becomes louder than the world's noise and stronger than your doubts.

Use this section for personal study, discipleship, or journaling.

These verses built this book — now let them make you.

Old Testament

Genesis 1:27 – God created man in His image → *Day 24 – The Strength of Servanthood*

Genesis 22:18 – All nations blessed through obedience → *Day 30 – Finish the Race*

Exodus 14:14 – "The LORD will fight for you" → *Day 7 – Faith Under Fire*

Exodus 20:3 – No other gods before Me → *Day 9 – Freedom Requires Faith*

Deuteronomy 6:5 – Love the LORD your God with all your heart → *Day 16 – Stay on the Narrow Way*

Joshua 1:9 – "Be strong and courageous" → *Day 27 – Courage in the Fire*

2 Samuel 22:31 – God's Word proves true → *Day 28 – The Power of God's Word*

Psalm 1:1–3 – Delight in the law of the LORD → *Day 8 – Purpose in the Pain*

Psalm 23:4 – Even though I walk through the valley → *Day 20 – Defiant Hope*

Psalm 37:4 – Delight yourself in the LORD → *Day 34 – Purpose Over Pleasure*

Psalm 46:10 – "Be still and know that I am God" → *Day 22 – The Power of Quiet Strength*

Psalm 119:105 – Your word is a lamp to my feet → *Day 28 – The Power of God's Word*

Psalm 127:3–5 – Children are a heritage from the LORD → *Letter 3 – To the Father Raising Warriors*

Proverbs 3:5–6 – Trust in the LORD with all your heart → *Day 13 – Wisdom in the Wilderness*

Proverbs 4:23 – Guard your heart → *Day 3 – Guard Your Heart*

Proverbs 13:20 – Walk with the wise → *Day 6 – The Company You Keep*

Proverbs 27:17 – Iron sharpens iron → *Day 6 – The Company You Keep*

Isaiah 40:31 – Those who wait on the LORD renew their strength → *Day 11 – When God Says Wait*

Isaiah 43:2 – When you walk through fire, you shall not be burned → *Day 27 – Courage in the Fire*

Jeremiah 29:11 – Plans to prosper you and not harm you → *Day 9 – Freedom Requires Faith*

New Testament

Matthew 5:9 – Blessed are the peacemakers → *Day 24 – The Strength of Servanthood*

Matthew 6:33 – Seek first the Kingdom → *Day 34 – Purpose Over Pleasure*

Matthew 7:13–14 – Enter by the narrow gate → *Day 16 – Stay on the Narrow Way*

Matthew 11:28–30 – Come to Me all who labor → *Day 5 – Discipline Over Desire*

Matthew 25:21 – "Well done, good and faithful servant" → *Day 37 – A Life Worth Remembering*

Luke 9:23 – Take up your Cross daily → *Day 26 – Faith That Moves Mountains*

John 11:25 – "I am the resurrection and the life" → *Day 1 – Jesus Defeated Death So You Can Live*

John 14:6 – "I am the way, and the truth, and the life" → *Day 2 – Truth Is Not Relative*

John 15:5 – Apart from Me you can do nothing → *Day 18 – We All Fall Short*

Romans 5:3–5 – Suffering produces endurance → *Day 8 – Purpose in the Pain*

Romans 8:28 – All things work together for good → *Day 15 – We Are Pilgrims, Not Residents*

Romans 12:2 – Be transformed by renewing your mind → *Day 25 – Guard Your Mind*

1 Corinthians 9:24 – Run in such a way as to obtain the prize → *Day 30 – Finish the Race*

1 Corinthians 13:4–7 – Love is patient and kind → *Letter 8 – To the Husband Learning to Lead with Love*

2 Corinthians 12:9 – "My grace is sufficient for you" → *Day 4 – Strength in Humility*

Galatians 5:1 – For freedom Christ has set us free → *Day 9 – Freedom Requires Faith*

Ephesians 5:25 – Husbands, love your wives → *Day 19 – Conviction Is Contagious*

Ephesians 6:10–11 – Put on the armor of God → *Day 7 – Faith Under Fire*

Philippians 1:6 – He who began a good work in you → *Day 31 – The Pursuit Continues*

Philippians 3:14 – Press on toward the goal → *Day 30 – Finish the Race*

Philippians 4:6–7 – Do not be anxious about anything → *Day 5 – Discipline Over Desire*

Colossians 3:23 – Work heartily, as for the Lord → *Day 12 – The Weight of Integrity*

2 Timothy 4:7 – I have fought the good fight → *Day 30 – Finish the Race*

Hebrews 10:23 – Hold fast the confession of our hope → *Day 20 – Defiant Hope*

Hebrews 12:1–2 – Run with endurance → *Day 30 – Finish the Race*

James 1:2–4 – Testing of faith produces steadfastness → *Letter 7 – To the Brother Who Refuses to Quit*

James 1:22 – Be doers of the word → *Reflection Day 1 – Wisdom in Action*

1 Peter 5:7 – Cast your anxieties on Him → *Day 23 – Forgiven to Forgive*

Revelation 2:10 – Be faithful unto death → *Day 30 – Finish the Race*

Made in the USA
Middletown, DE
14 December 2025